TH‾

___OF___
THE FOLD

IN
THE SHELTER
OF
THE FOLD

A second collection of parables from farm life
in the Welsh mountains

John & Mari Jones

Translated from the Welsh by
Mrs Bethan Lloyd-Jones

BRYNTIRION PRESS

248
JON

Scripture quotations are taken from the Holy Bible, New
International Version. Copyright ©1973, 1978, 1984 by
International Bible Society. Used by permission of Hodder
and Stoughton Limited.

Designed by Tony Cantale Graphics
Illustrations by Rhiain M. Davies and Pat Ware
Photographs (apart from the photograph of John Jones) by
W. Arvon Williams
Cover design by Rhiain M. Davies
Cover photograph by Ann Gruffydd Rhys

These stories first appeared in book form in the Welsh-
language edition of this book, entitled *Yng Nghysgod y
Gorlan*, which was published in 1979.

Published by Bryntirion Press
Bryntirion, Bridgend CF31 4DX
Printed by Gomer Press, Llandysul

CONTENTS

Photographs

1
PERSISTENCE

Before a winter storm, as surely as anything, the sheep in the meadows can be seen playing together as though the vitality of youth has returned to their heels. They are nimble lambs again, leaping and frolicking and leaving quite a space between their hind quarters and the earth beneath them!

Why do they shake their bodies like this? Is it in order to warm themselves up against the keen breeze that precedes the storm? Or have they some deep prophetic instinct that eventually drives them relentlessly to the shelter of the hedges?

The mountain sheep have a different way of letting us know that a snowstorm awaits us. They come down in good time from the heights and crowd together in the sheltered places or make for the boundary between the enclosed pasture and the open mountain. When a storm threatens, the shepherd likes to take a turn in the mountain to see exactly where the sheep have gathered. Before morning they may well be buried under a blanket of snow. The very safety of the creatures depends on their attention and obedience to their instincts. They are governed by their nature.

This is what accounts for their unyielding perseverance. When the threatening snowstorms continually drape the mountains, then the sheep, huddled at the boundary fences, look at us pitifully, as though earnestly pleading their cause to be allowed into the lower pastures. We ignore them for as long as possible, until we realize at last that they will not give up. If they do not get their way, they will starve, for nothing else will make them move.

This year we had mercy on them and yielded to their persistence. We opened the mountain gates and let them come down a whole month earlier than usual. And oh! the satisfaction of those sheep as they tasted the green grass of the fields, the grass usually reserved for the time when they become heavy with lamb!

Later in the season there was a change in the weather and it grew warmer. Now they should really go back for a while to the open mountain, if only to give time for the spring pasturage to grow in the fields. But sheep know nothing of the problem caused by a lack of sufficient grass at that time.

One sunny afternoon I went with John to try to drive the sheep over Craig y Pistyll Gwyn ('White Waterfall Rock') back again to the mountain pasture. He intended to follow the sheep up the steep path beside the waterfall, pointing out another path for me to follow, a little further back, to the top of the rock. By going that way I could get ahead of the sheep and turn them back, should they decide to turn tail and go down again.

Although I could trace the path clearly looking up from below – I could see the whole pattern from a distance, from its beginning to the top of the rock – yet as I climbed, I lost sight of it and found myself continually doubting whether I was on the right track. This spoilt much of the pleasure of our joint effort. What a misery uncertainty is – wondering all the time whether I was pushing on to no purpose and whether or not I would, in the end, reach the right spot on top of the rock. This made me dawdle too much and lose my enthusiasm. Whenever I looked up and saw the climb ahead of me, I came near to giving up. Between that, the uncertainty, and the breathlessness due to lack of exercise, and being spoilt by walking so much on the flat, I hardly had the heart to go on.

Suddenly it dawned upon me that I would get nowhere like this, and that climb I must, with the same determination not to go back as possessed the sheep in their desire to come down. Realizing this, I took courage and went on – one step at a time, no looking up, putting out of my mind the steepness of the path and the stiff climb ahead, comforting myself with the thought that each time I placed one foot above the other, I was one step nearer the goal, and I could greet the top of the rock, when I reached there, like Newman in his hymn:

> *Keep Thou my feet; I do not ask to see*
> *The distant scene: one step enough for me.*

I reached the top of the rock at last, but oh! after all my efforts, the sheep had got there before me! The determined wretches had turned back, gone round in a circle and were now going full tilt for the lowlands once more.

It is a hopeless task to try to persuade sheep to leave their good grazing for something less tasty. Once they have tasted the better and found their appetite deeply satisfied, it requires a great effort to wean them from the desire for more and to get them to forget that flavour. This is what accounts for the dogged obstinacy of the sheep. And who can refuse them? They were allowed to continue their feasting in the lower pastures until lambing time and afterwards.

Isn't this very much like the parable of the friend who came at midnight asking for bread?

'I tell you, though he will not get up and give him the bread because he is his friend, yet because of the man's persistence he will get up and give him as much as he needs. So I say to you: Ask and it will be given to you; seek and you will find; knock and the door will be opened to you . . . If you then, though you are evil, know how to give good gifts to your children, how much more will your Father in heaven give the Holy Spirit to those who ask him!'
Luke 11:8-9,13

2
FLY AND HER MASTER

'I'm off to the National Eisteddfod this year,' said Hefin, who helps us with the farm work. The rain had kept off and the bales of hay were dry and sweet in the safety of the rickyard. And as they had been harvested in the heat of the sun, the smell of them reminded us of a batch of bread, straight from the oven!

As he said goodbye to us that morning, Hefin entrusted to us the care of his dogs.

There never was a better example of faithfulness than little Fly in her relationship with her master. He is always talking to her, and has done so throughout the years, for Fly is old now; and this, no doubt, has strengthened the bond between them. If Hefin has to make a trip with the tractor she is allowed to sit on his knee, and indeed she is often to be seen on the tractor when it is at work. But when the steep places are being ploughed and great care is needed, she is not then allowed to be a passenger. Instead, as the furrows are formed, the little dog will follow the plough consistently up and down the field.

As, sooner or later, tiredness comes to the little legs, she will go to meet the tractor three-quarters of the way up the field and then follow it down. Later, the walk will be shortened to half-way up the field; but she keeps on going, up and down. Before the end of the afternoon, the walk up the field has to be cut to a quarter, and in the end she has to be satisfied with lying on his coat – Hefin's coat and none other! – in the corner of the field.

If she finds her master still for a minute, even in the middle of his work, Fly never stops licking him – his hands, his arms, his neck, his face, in a manifestation of her love for him, never taking her eyes off him. She cannot bear him out of her sight. There is no-one else in little Fly's world – Hefin is her life.

Fly is not particularly brilliant in her work. She never accomplishes anything great. But she is obedient in the little things. She performs the small duties well, and her greatest virtue is that she is always there when she is needed. Where her master is, there will Fly be. She is of value because she will do what is necessary at the right moment – before the whole flock of sheep disappears through some forbidden opening, for instance! By the time the call has gone out and been answered by some of the other dogs, who are possibly on the trail of some enticing carcass, the damage has been done – and how much greater the work of restoring order then! 'A near neighbour is better than a far friend,' says the old proverb.

* * * * *

Living always, as she does, within sight of the idol of her heart, what a tragedy it was for poor little Fly not to be allowed to share the delights of the Eisteddfod with him! She had to be left at home, not to bark, but to howl her mournful, longing heart-break. She would not be comforted; nothing and nobody else would do. She was in the depths of misery every day until the return of her idol and her sunshine. Oh! the welcome that she gave him! All the dust of the Eisteddfod was licked clean in no time.

The old saints of our chapels and churches in the past were very much like this. 'If any man serve me, let him follow me; and where I am, there shall also my servant be' (John 12:26). Their walk was close to their Saviour, and should the relationship between them be clouded at times, they were conscious at once of the loss of the divine presence, so precious was it to them. We find them on their knees, broken and in fervent supplication until the blessing returns and they taste again the heavenly powers.

God in His sovereignty would sometimes hold back the blessing for a time, giving a sense of need to remind His people that He alone has the right to give and to withhold the divine visitations, and to prove that they are not the fruit of man's efforts either. And yet, when He sees such deep consciousness of need and the insistent longing for Him, God cannot long delay the gracious visitations without answering in His own way and time. He well knows the welcome He will receive when He comes.

3
ACKNOWLEDGED WITH THANKS

It is interesting to observe the postures assumed by the various animals; they can be quite significant. Take, for instance, the attitude of the hen and her kind as they quench their thirst. After every sip the hen looks upward. She gives the impression that she is gratefully acknowledging the source of her satisfaction. Taking another sip, and then another, she repeats the action again and again.

But the pig has little to teach us. Burrowing under the oaks for acorns in the autumn, he snorts and grunts his way from one acorn to another like a vacuum cleaner. Everything disappears into his stomach without a single upward glance of acknowledgment to the Giver. He slogs away at his food without a thought; filling his belly is his only interest.

*   *   *   *   *

When a horse wants to lie down, he first of all folds his hind legs – and flop! down he goes all of a heap, tucking his front legs clumsily beneath him. When he gets up again, the hind legs come up first; then a heave, and the front legs are up under him. The reason for this, apparently, is that the backward kick of the horse is his means of self-defence.

The way of the sheep, and of the cow also, is much more graceful. They both go on their knees first as they prepare to lie down, and the same again when they get up – they meekly bend their knees. Though the earth be bare, and the grazing around them often poor, they do not change their thankful attitude. Occasionally a cow will decide to lie down and to get up in some other way, and all her life she will appear clumsy and awkward. A sick cow, in spite of her weakness, is able to get on to her feet wonderfully well if she goes on her knees first. Indeed, many a cow has died in her weakness by failing to go on her knees first in order to get up.

'But ask the animals, and they will teach you; or the birds of the air, and they will tell you.'
Job 12:7

Lift thy hands, thy knees down bending,
On Christ's face thine eyes attending;
Seek His strength, His grace, His bounty,
Christ extolling, kneeling humbly.

VICAR PRICHARD (tr.)

4
SERMONS
IN TREES

'How did you get on?' and 'What caused it?'

Those were the questions we asked each other for days after the devastating gale that struck us – questions which often recurred as we trod twigs and small pieces of slate underfoot.

Recently, in order to widen one stretch of the main road, it had been necessary to remove a whole row – the outer row – of the evergreen trees of the forest, and we remarked on how well-rooted they were. Since they were the ones that nearly always had to face the very teeth of the storms, they had had to push their roots deep down for strength.

At the same time they kindly sheltered the rest of the trees, and so there was no need for these to waste their strength in rooting deep. They seemed to live a superficial life, concentrating their growth upwards in search of light; they did not even bother to throw out branches, except at their tops. Wherever any form of life is found, there is always a striving after light. But they were all flung down like matchwood by the storm. How sad we were next day to see the area denuded!

Not only these, but many old trees also fell prey to the storm, and came down headlong before it – trees that had survived many a shaking before this. Every tree spreads its strongest roots in the direction of the prevailing wind; but this time the wind came from an unexpected quarter, and they were struck at their weakest point, the spot they had neglected to guard. This storm had tested both the young trees, not deeply rooted, and also the older, unprepared ones.

Near the road below our house stood a great ash tree The point where the trunk divided into two main branches seemed to invite the rain to loiter there, with the obvious result that it caused rot to set in. One of these mighty branches came crashing down across the road, putting a stop to all traffic for a while. There is no doubt that the other branch will follow. Little did we know of this weakness until it was put to the test by the storm.

It does not take a great storm to bring down a diseased or cankerous tree.

'So, if you think you are standing firm, be careful that you don't fall!'
   1 Corinthians 10:12

'Brothers, if someone is caught in a sin, you who are spiritual should restore him gently. But watch yourself, or you also may be tempted.'
   Galatians 6:1

5
THE SHEPHERD

The poet Pedrog, in his winning 'Ode to the Shepherd' at
the National Eisteddfod held in Liverpool in 1900, asks
what would become of sheep without a shepherd. Well,
indeed, what *would* become of sheep without a shepherd?
– if only at lambing time, for example. A sheep may be in
difficulties, and how important it is that someone should
be there at the time to shorten the tediousness of the
labour, and often, indeed, to save life. 'It is impossible to
get round them all often enough' is the complaint of
every shepherd in the spring.

It seems that there is a whole host of enemies ready
to take advantage of so defenceless a little creature as a
lamb – foxes, dogs, crows, as well as storms and cruel

weather. 'Pretty, innocent, tame and harmless things of earth,' the poet Eifion Wyn calls them. Their only protection, apart from the shepherd, is a dam of strong character, one who can recognize the danger from afar, and can withstand it boldly, stamping her feet and thumping the ground for her very life – and that is all the poor thing *can* do.

Again, who but the shepherd will take the lamb back to its mother? It can push its head and its little body quite happily through the hole in the hedge; and then it will wander further and further away, out of reach of its mother's cry. But how to find the hole in the hedge and get back again? Ah! that is much harder.

The lambs, naturally enough, get special attention from every shepherd. He likes to see an abundance of healthy lambs, for they are the hope of the flock for the future. He will take good care that the land where the ewe lambs are to spend their first winter and their season of growth is in good condition. A dry and wholesome place is best, for a damp site may harbour a certain snail which will attack a lamb's liver. If there is the slightest doubt, an injection is the only safeguard – for in a very short time these snails can do great harm to the young, and even kill them.

It must always be remembered that the natural habitat of the Welsh sheep is the mountain, and so their freedom should not be too restricted – within reason, of course. Their natural requirement is to have plenty of land underfoot. If they do not get it they will react to this later on. If they are not given opportunity for the natural development of their bodies, they will have difficulties with lambing when the time comes.

The key to the shepherd's success is his constant care of the feeble ones, and his quickness to notice any that are losing ground. The secret is to give these special attention, and that in good time. It is a custom with some owners, during the winter months, to gather the sheep together at monthly intervals, in order to separate the weak ones from among them and to put these apart in a richer pasture especially prepared for them.

To keep the sheep happy and contented in their own territory, the home grazing must be good. And good grazing also helps to get them in good condition to meet the winter storms, and to ensure reserves of strength when the spring brings on the troubles and crises of lambing time. Good pasture actually lessens the work of shepherding; a sheep that is not satisfied with its own, will always be looking over the boundary at some other pasture. To the sheep, the grass on the other side of the boundary always seems better and greener, and once they get a taste for wandering, it is very difficult to get them to settle down.

When, as often happens, the natural elements seem once more to be fighting against them, and the sheep are buried under a heavy fall of snow – some perhaps carrying their lambs, and all hungry to the point of starvation, with the snow weighing heavily upon them – their only hope then is that the shepherd will find them and rescue them from their misery by clearing a pathway through the snow, setting them free once more.

What is it that makes a shepherd risk his life to rescue a sheep from a cleft or a ledge in the rock? If he is a born shepherd, it will not be the value of the sheep, in terms of its market price, that spurs him on to muster all his energies to counteract the results of its foolish inclination to stray.

I heard of a shepherd in this district, whose mountain pasture land included one very rocky part. During one severe storm of wind and snow, his sheep were swept to the very edge of a rocky precipice. Soon, great drifts of snow blocked their way back over the mountain top, and before them yawned the precipice.

The shepherd knew that the only hope of saving them lay in the young shepherd boy going behind the flock and driving them very slowly and carefully along the narrow strip between the snowdrift and the precipice. Meanwhile he himself would stand on the rocky edge of the drop, to keep the sheep from going over. He knew that if they were to panic and rush and push against him as they went by, he could well lose his balance and be hurled headlong onto the rocks below.

What, we may wonder, was the compulsion behind this brave act? In spite of careful shepherding and the best possible feeding, sheep are thoughtless enough creatures and they are slow to show any appreciation – in contrast to the horse or the dog, for instance. Why then does the shepherd battle on and persevere in spite of seeing no manifestation or acknowledgment of gratitude? Eifion Wyn answers the question in part of his 'Ode to the Shepherd':

> *The yoke of his daily task seems light to him,*
> *The spread of the mountain land no weariness.*
> *The greater the load, the heavier it be, the son*
> *   of the soil is*
> *True to his stock – **he loves his own.***

EIFION WYN (tr.)

'*He loves his own*' – that is the secret.

'I am the good shepherd. The good shepherd lays down his life for the sheep. The hired hand is not the shepherd who owns the sheep. So when he sees the wolf coming, he abandons the sheep and runs

away. Then the wolf attacks the flock and scatters it. The man runs away because he is a hired hand and cares nothing for the sheep.'
John 10:11-13

What brought Him from the courts of glory
Of His own will to sorrow's country?
What brought Him to the hill Golgotha?
'Twas love unbounded – Hallelujah!

THOMAS JONES, DENBIGH (tr.)

6
BALANCE

It always gives me great pleasure when Cae Fron ('The Field on the Slope') is re-sown, for it lies only a few yards from the kitchen window. My interest was aroused again this year as I watched the seemingly endless preparations for the sowing. The careful ploughing of the whole field came first, and then harrowing the soil into a fine tilth. Next came feeding it with the necessary chemicals, in order to make up for any and every deficiency found in it; then spreading it over with 'basic slag' to raise the percentage of phosphates, and then adding a compound to bring the nitrogen and potash up to the required level. And all this to make an acceptable bed to suit the growing requirements of the 'rape' seeds, which will provide one year's green growth to fatten the lambs, and the grass seeds, which it is hoped will be a continuous growth.

We kept an anxious eye on it all during this year's hot summer. What, we wondered, would become of the seed in such a steeply sloping field – a field lying in the full glare of the sun the whole day through? It was very hard on the seeds at times and they had to fight for their lives. Yet I marvelled at how well they grew.

It was interesting to watch the first batch of lambs that were allowed to feast on the new growth. Naturally enough, we looked forward to seeing them taking to it greedily at the first go, but we were amazed to see them eating it very sparingly and cautiously. I had thought that once they had their teeth into such a tasty delicacy, they would have rushed at it for more. How quickly they were satisfied!

Before long, in spite of the goodness and richness of the food spread around them, we could see them thrusting their heads under the hedges, as though they were looking for some tasty bits to eat there! What could there be that they were unable to find in the new growth?

From their persistence in searching, it was obvious that their bodies were calling for something else, something that was missing from the rich grass at hand, something that their instincts told them was essential for their bodily well-being. Doubtless the plough, in turning the sods over, had deprived them of the very thing that they were now searching for. Good though the chemicals were, the lambs showed us plainly that the one thing, the missing item for which they were looking, was to be found in the strip around the field – that strip of land alongside the hedges where the plough could not reach.

In the end we had to open the gate into another field, so that they could graze on the old grass as well as the new. There they spent half their time, picking here and there between intervals of resting – picking the odd blade which was most to their taste and which they knew they needed. It was easy to see that they could take but very little at a time of the protein contained in the new green growth. Had they been filled with this concentrated food, very soon their stomachs would shrink, and that would mean less need to go searching for food, and more resting-time for the rich food to produce more flesh. So it was essential for them to search for and find this scarce necessity to be added to their diet in good time before they were too full.

In the past we have had some quite avoidable losses among the dams and the ewes in lamb through keeping them too long on ploughed and re-sown land. Because they did not get a balanced diet in the new growth, and because at the same time the lambs were a steady drain on them, these poor mothers would suddenly to all appearances become unconscious. Then what a rush to catch them before they breathed their last! They would, according to the signs and symptoms, be given an injection of calcium or magnesium as the case might be. It would be warmed up hastily to the temperature of the sheep's blood, in case it proved too great a shock to its system. It is wonderful how quickly they recover, once the deficiency in their system is made up. They revive from minute to minute, and they will be on their feet again in no time. And the thing that humbles us every time is the realization that they would have searched themselves for the leaf that would have made up the deficiency, had it been anywhere within their reach.

I find myself asking whether it is possible that the animals know what is best for them, better than man knows what is best for him. Man will pursue what he likes best at the time, whether it is good for him or not. The animal will not go against its instincts; it will search, in so far as it is possible, for what is essential to its well-being. But, with all his so-called wisdom, man will ignore the greatest need in his life – the need for God.

We can fill our lives with things, which, in themselves, are good and lawful enough. We can also fill our heads with correct and orthodox knowledge – and our hearts still be weak and feeble and cold towards God. 'Only one thing is needed', said the Lord Jesus Christ, 'and Mary has chosen what is better' – that is, to know Him aright and to grow in that knowledge. Without that, the richest food and the best doctrinal teaching can become a burden to the soul, and lethal in the end. There must be, in life, a balance of understanding and emotion, of doctrine and experience.

> 'The ox knows his master, the donkey his owner's manger, but Israel does not know, my people do not understand.'
> Isaiah 1:3

7
BLODWEN

'I said goodbye to a real Christian of a cow today,' said John half-humorously, having just sold Blodwen in the mart at Dolgellau. She will be sorely missed in the cowshed and the yard too. If one of the other cows should try to pick a quarrel with her, Blodwen would always retreat. With her great horns, shaped like the handle-bars of a bicycle, powerful and pointed, it would have been child's play for her to toss over her shoulder any creature that dared annoy her. But she was very gentle, and would always look kindly at you with her big eyes.

She was a good mother to her offspring, with a generous udder; easy to milk, Blodwen knew nothing of the trick of withholding her milk. She was easy to manage too, and never objected to the captivity of the cow-collar, nor would she rush to freedom when she was loosed from it. Leisurely and graceful in her movements, she never raised a foot – except to move from one place to another. She gave of her best to everyone. She was just the kind that many would put squarely in heaven – the animal heaven! – without hesitation at her journey's end.

She had her excellent pedigree to thank for her equable temperament; her mother was exactly the same. Should another cow, longing to be like her in nature and to possess the same tranquillity, ask for her help to attain this, Blodwen would not be able to help her. All she could say would be, 'You should have chosen better parents – parents to be proud of!'

That is how she was born, and since then she had received nothing from the outside, either from her master or anybody else. All her good qualities were inherent in her nature.

No, in spite of all her virtues, Blodwen is not a true picture of the Christian. As the animals differ one from another, so among men we find some pleasant and others not so pleasant. These are natural differences. But is not the life of the Christian something that comes to him from outside of himself? It is not his own nature refined, but the gift of a new nature.

It is grace that makes a man a Christian, not his own virtues. And we *receive* grace rather than inherit it. We receive a new life through believing in the Lord Jesus Christ.

'Therefore, if anyone is in Christ, he is a new
creation; the old has gone, the new has come!'
`2 Corinthians 5:17

'Yet to all who received him, to those who believed
in his name, he gave the right to become children of
God – children born not of natural descent, nor of
human decision or a husband's will, but born of
God.'
John 1:12-13

8
RECOGNITION

In one of the fields furthest away from the house a ewe stands over her lamb, unable to persuade herself that there is no life in it. Troublesome things often happen in remote places. It is essential to get the ewe and her dead lamb down to the barn. If she is to take to another lamb, the dead lamb must be skinned, and the skin draped over the lamb that she is to adopt.

The easiest and best way to get the ewe to the barn is to tie the legs of the dead lamb together with a good length of binder cord, and for someone either on foot or on horseback to drag it along the ground behind him. It is remarkable how the woolly mother will follow the tracks of her dead lamb. Every now and then she is given the opportunity to sniff the little corpse, just to reassure

herself. She will follow for half a mile or more, going straight through a flock of other sheep and lambs, until at last she comes, close behind it, to the barn. Draping the live lamb, probably a little orphan, in her own lamb's skin is what will persuade her that it is her own and she will adopt it.

*   *   *   *   *

In another field there is a ewe with twin lambs. One of them has wandered away from her; mingling with the other lambs, it has heedlessly strayed further and further away – a thing which often happens. It has followed them into the adjoining field and is now out of earshot of its mother's call. How much easier it is to stray than to find the way back! Mealtime comes and its mother is not there. The other lambs are sucking away in turn, and it tries hard to get a surreptitious gulp from one sheep after another, only to be refused every time – a good thump from one and all, and a 'Go to your own mother!' But 'Where is she?' is the question.

By this time, alas, it will have rubbed itself a good deal against the other sheep and lambs, and when it finds its mother, perhaps after quite a time, the tragedy is that she will reject it. She will sniff it carefully, over and over, from nose to tail, and her doubts are obvious. By this time it has an alien smell; it smells of the others against which it has been rubbing. The result is that she gives all her attention to the lamb that never left her side, in spite of the fact that the other has come back to her, bleating pitifully and trying to stake its claim. But no, it is not allowed to suck. The bleating and the smell have to be the two-fold guarantee that it is truly her own lamb.

The three of them have to be brought to the barn, and the lamb that has never left her side taken from her for a while. Then she and the lamb that she doubts are put together in a confined corner between bales of straw, so that his woolly coat will rub against hers, and the strange smell – and all doubts – be dispelled. It also helps to hold her frequently so that the lamb may suck – it is wonderful how a sheep will take to a lamb to whom she can *give*. She will grow to love one that sucks consistently from her and is dependent upon her; this seems to generate a bond of acceptance between them. At this stage it is safe to bring the other twin to her; now the two of them can share equally in their woolly heritage.

Although animals are usually so quick to recognize their own, they can sometimes lose all knowledge of their straying offspring. But the Word of God tells us plainly of One who, without fail and in all circumstances, knows His own and is always ready to welcome the repentant wanderer.

'I am the good shepherd; I know my sheep and my sheep know me.'
John 10:14

9
CONTINUITY

What is there to compare with autumn colouring for sheer
beauty? Especially in a valley like ours, where so many
varieties of trees are crowded together. Each tree seems to
be doing everything in its power to show all the beauty
that it can, before calling back the sap from sprigs and
branches to invest it in itself until the spring. The whole
scene is awash with colour, pale and dark yellows melting
into one another in the breeze, while we feast our eyes in
utter contentment on the charm of it all.

One night of sharp frost, and yet another season of
colourful beauty has vanished. Here and there, perhaps,
an occasional young tree may hold on more tightly to its
leaves for a while – only to follow the others before long.
'What a waste of all that growth!' we may think to
ourselves, as we plough a path for our feet through deep

layers of withered leaves. Very soon the whole dry and shrivelled harvest of them will be blown and scattered by the wind to the base of the hedges and to oblivion.

But no! that is not the end of them. The death of one season's growth is but a source of manure and nourishment for the continuance of growth in another season – just as the rotting compost in our gardens becomes a valuable manure for the future.

* * * * *

It is the colour, form and scent of petals that arouse our admiration, and these are the things that lure the bees to collect the pollen. The seed pods get little of our attention. But after the beauty fades and disappears, it is upon these, the maturing seeds, that the continuation of the species will depend. The beauty does not exist for our own sake, but to make it possible for the plant to reproduce itself for the future. Where there is life there is hope of its continuance.

* * * * *

When dealing with the government, the farmer will plead for a long-term policy in determining prices, so that he may plan his work scheme. But he knows that with regard to nature he can make his plans without any anxiety, so reliable and infallible is she. Though seasons vary, they come regularly in their turn, one pushing the other out of the way, one reaping the other's harvest. Everything seems to reflect the spin of the earth itself – that continuous turning that gives us so reliably our day and night, our summer and winter.

The marvellous consistency and continuity found in nature seem to be doing their best to convince us of the most important thing, and the very greatest – that God is good in all His works.

> 'Or do you show contempt for the riches of his kindness, tolerance and patience, not realising that God's kindness leads you towards repentance?'
>   Romans 2:4

> 'Men, why are you doing this? We too are only men, human like you. We are bringing you good news, telling you to turn from these worthless things to the living God, who made heaven and earth and sea and everything in them. In the past, he let all nations go their own way. Yet he has not left himself without testimony: He has shown kindness by giving you rain from heaven and crops in their seasons; he provides you with plenty of food and fills your hearts with joy.'
>   Acts 14:15-17

10
A BETTER TIME
TO COME

Every living thing has to come face to face with death.
That is the basis of the fear that characterizes every
creature. It is usually quite an undertaking to approach an
animal in order to tame it, and to get it to put aside its
fear. Though you tiptoe lightly, it is no mean feat to lay
your hand on a little lamb fast asleep in the field, or to get

near a tomtit that comes to pick away at the corners of your windows. They only need to see your shadow, and off they go for their lives – yes! for their lives.

It is this innate fear that causes defenceless creatures like the sheep and the cow to chew the cud. All animals have some God-given means of protecting themselves, and this is theirs. It enables them to graze hastily, sending their food half-digested into their stomachs. Then, when they have had enough, and feel satisfied that all is safe and quiet, they will bring back the food to be chewed and re-chewed at their leisure, and in comparative freedom from all dangers and disturbances.

Every creature seems to live in this kind of fear. The only safety for the worms and insects in the soil is to keep out of the way of the mole. If the earthworm shows the tip of his nose above ground, some hen or other bird will see in him a nice piece of ham for breakfast. If chicken is on his menu for dinner, the crafty-eyed fox will lose no opportunity to catch and gobble one up. How cruel the animals are to each other! It is no wonder that there is some instinct in them which tells them that there is a better time to come. 'We know that the whole creation has been groaning as in the pains of childbirth right up to the present time' (Romans 8:22).

* * * * *

After reclaiming an area of mountain land, clearing away the bracken and scrub – 'raising green pasture on the face of desert earth' as Alun Mabon did in Ceiriog's poem – it is indeed a sad picture to see that it has all been in vain! Without a constant struggle to keep old growth at bay in order to give the new a chance, it is all a waste of energy. In spite of the efficiency of the new chemicals, it is by 'the sweat of your brow' and the unyielding persistence of the tractor that 'you will eat your food'

(Genesis 3:19). 'Let the strongest oppress and the weakest cry' is what holds in the world of plants and animals.

Yes, the earth and all it contains, as well as man, came under condemnation as a result of the Fall in the Garden of Eden. Here, without a doubt, we have facts of life that man can never change, however much he may strive to do so.

* * * * *

It is not always an unmixed pleasure to live within this old body. Weariness and pain come soon enough on the journey. Indeed, some member or other may refuse to work at all. Even though the surgeon's treatment may restore its usefulness for a time, it will ultimately fail.

Man's soul and conscience become one with God when he is adopted as His child here on earth. But when we are raised from the dead in the image and likeness of Christ, the body as well as the soul will be changed into full perfection. In that day, that will be the story of the whole of creation – a new heaven and a new earth – and all fear in the animals will cease.

'I consider that our present sufferings are not worth comparing with the glory that will be revealed in us.'
  Romans 8:18

'We know that the whole creation has been groaning as in the pains of childbirth right up to the present time. Not only so, but we ourselves, who have the firstfruits of the Spirit, groan inwardly as we wait eagerly for our adoption as sons, the redemption of our bodies.'
  Romans 8:22-23

'The wolf will live with the lamb, the leopard will lie down with the goat, the calf and the lion and the yearling together; and a little child will lead them. The cow will feed with the bear, their young will lie down together, and the lion will eat straw like the ox. The infant will play near the hole of the cobra, and the young child put his hand into the viper's nest. They will neither harm nor destroy on all my holy mountain, for the earth will be full of the knowledge of the Lord as the waters cover the sea.'

Isaiah 11:6-9

11
THE CRY

She was a young two-year-old ewe, and she needed help to deliver her first lamb. The dogs had to be sent off to round her up several times before she was finally cornered. She little thought, in her obstinacy, that her capture was a favour. She was soon relieved of her burden and pain, and in no time at all that burden lay at her side – a little wet yellow bundle. But the wretch would take no notice of it, and as soon as she could, off she went, as though refusing to acknowledge any connection with it.

In spite of being brought back several times, she would take no notice of it – that poor defenceless little scrap, unable to win its mother's love. She was possibly upset by the new experience of giving birth for the first time, and that, together with the panic caused by the dogs, made her totally ignore her natural instincts.

There was nothing for it but to drive her with the help of the dogs to the barn, to corner her there and leave the lamb with her so that she could acquaint herself with it. As it happened, they were a long way from the house, and it was no small undertaking to carry a small unlicked lamb in one's arms, smothered as it was in yellow slime, straight from the womb! As a rule, the first thing that a sheep will do after dropping her lamb is to lick it all over, and then swallow the caul and the after-birth and all. In the wonderful order of nature, this is how the iron and some of the vitamins which her body gave the lamb while she was carrying it are returned to her.

As they came within sight of the barn, after walking about half a mile, the little lamb in John's arms gave a bleat – his very first cry. At that, his mother stood stock still, then suddenly she turned back and looked eagerly towards the lamb. That bleating cry awoke some innate instinct in the sheep, and she reacted as though a clock had struck within her. She responded at once. How wonderful! That bleat, which she had never heard before, told her with absolute certainty that it was her very own lamb.

John could not put the lamb down soon enough; she claimed it that very moment. They were left there together as quickly and as quietly as possible, and she did not leave its side until she had licked it clean. The last glimpse of them showed the lamb sucking away to its heart's content. There they were, an inseparable pair, with the lamb assured of all the love and care that a woolly mother can give to her offspring. John, filthy and wet to the skin, came back to the house, not only to wash himself and change his clothes, but to tell the story with joyful wonder.

All that the shepherd could do was to bring them, mother and lamb, together. That is also the work of every messenger of the truth, every servant of God. He is to bring the good news of the gospel to the ears of the people, to bring within their reach the good news of the salvation that is in the Lord Jesus Christ.

It was instinct that made the lamb bleat, and it was instinct that made the mother answer its cry. And it is an instinct, which God through His grace has planted in His children by the Holy Spirit, that awakens the cry, '*Abba, Father*', within us. When that happens, God never fails to answer. Then there will be relationship and fellowship, and we shall inherit all the love and the care which is in God for us.

'For you did not receive a spirit that makes you a slave again to fear, but you received the Spirit of sonship. And by him we cry, '*Abba*, Father.'
    Romans 8:15

> *Whence hath my desire been kindled?*
> *What hath made this cold heart burn?*
> *Whence the yearning for those objects*
> *Which before my soul did spurn?*
> *Jesus, Jesus,*
> *All, 'tis all Thy perfect work.*
> WILLIAM WILLIAMS, PANTYCELYN (tr.)

12
GROWTH

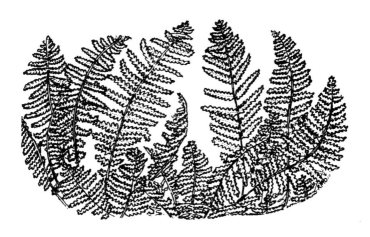

Recently we undertook the task of clearing a very steep area of the mountainside. A road was cut in the mountain above the spot to enable us to take the various fertilizers there. The bracken was first destroyed by means of some special chemicals sprayed from the air. Then the cleared land was broken to pieces – almost to dust – by a machine suitable for the work. Then was added an adequate complement of lime and all the other things necessary to make up for the natural deficiencies of the soil.

What a sweaty time that was! The bags of lime had to be dragged to the appropriate spots and their contents spread with spades; everything was done to give the grass seed the chance of germinating in favourable conditions.

Now, with the seeding finished, since the slope was too steep for a harrow to be used, a flock of sheep had to be walked back and forth over the ground. As their feet sank into the ground, they buried the seed deep in the earth. The next day, and for the following two days after the sowing, there fell a gentle, warm rain which made the soil conditions ideal for stirring awake the life that lay within the seed. Everything looked good, with the promise of success for the reclamation, and the seed began to grow hopefully.

But this was the last rain to fall for weeks! The seed could have kept quite well in the soil for a long time had it been dry from the outset, but once the dampness had inspired growth, it had to go on growing. Having begun to grow, this seed had a hard time on the dry mountain slopes.

In this, the seed is different from the potato, which can live for a long time on its own resources. But even with the potato, once the shoots have taken all the nourishment out of it, and have left the empty skin aside to die, then the environment becomes important to the potato too, for the roots will now depend on the state of the soil for their moisture and their very lives. Like the seed, the potato will be dependent on its environment, either to go on growing, or to shrivel and die. Once the life in the seed is awakened it *must* continue to grow, or cease to exist.

Death was the end of the story for the seed that began to sprout on the mountain slope. One season's growth of rape could have succeeded in conquering the drought, because it has roots which penetrate deeply. But as for the smaller seeds, the seeds of the grass that we expected to be there permanently, they did not root more deeply than the earth which we had worked, and that loose soil very soon dried up, as it could not hold the moisture. We shall have to go through the whole costly process again – at least in part – and re-seed the area.

It is a tragedy to see the awakening of new life in the heart of man, and not see that life nurtured in a warm, loving, spiritually-alive Christian atmosphere.

Is not this why William Willams, Pantycelyn, asks in one of his hymns:

Why should flowers just appearing
Fail from thirst and early want?
Lead forthwith refreshing showers
That give strength to grow with might,
One sweet shower in the morning,
Also one at evening light.

tr. R.R. WILLIAMS

'But blessed is the man who trusts in the Lord, whose confidence is in him. He will be like a tree planted by the water that sends out its roots by the stream. It does not fear when heat comes; its leaves are always green. It has no worries in a year of drought and never fails to bear fruit.'

Jeremiah 17:7-8

13
THE BROOK

'I'll come with you' is the usual response when anyone declares his intention of going to see Ceunant y Felin ('The Mill Gorge'), not far from this farm of ours.

'Do be careful; it's terribly dangerous when it's wet. Take hold of this or that. Slowly now, or you'll slip.'

It is in the sound of such warnings that one goes down to see the waterfall.

Once there, we are at once reminded of others who have been there before us to enjoy the same sight. They had lingered long enough to carve their names to the accompaniment of the music of falling water – to carve their names deeply in the rock behind us, together with the year of their visit – dates that take us back to the end of the eighteenth century.

This is where the Pumrhyd brook pours its waters, emptying itself unsparingly, knowing nothing of what will become of it. Every drop of water that comes in its turn to the brink of the rock has to make the same leap into the unknown. Each one for itself goes trustfully over the edge, not knowing that the steady flow over countless years has hollowed out several basins in the rock which, like loving arms, hold the waters and break their fall, saving them from plunging to the bottom in a single leap.

This is a sight that thrills me whenever I see it – the sight of the white foaming water falling from hollow to hollow, each new troughful pushing its predecessor over the edge.

To see the brook merrily resuming its song on reaching the foot of the cliff is sheer delight. It is not a murmurous singing, like the mountain stream in Ceiriog's well-known Welsh poem, but a song of rejoicing, bubbling over with hallelujahs in thankfulness for having come victoriously through the ordeal of venturing into the unknown.

The waters of the brook are much clearer now. Is it possible that it was washing its waters in the white foam? Was there some separation there between the waters of the brook and the clinging earth that had been so much a part of it before the great purification in the turbulence of the waterfall?

The water is so crystal-clear that the bed of the stream can be seen quite clearly now – a kind of bright transparent purity. There is little fear of moss or any other weed flourishing in its bed any more. There is too much movement and pushing forward of the waters, as though some new source of energy were behind them.

How different from the pools we see in some streams! In these it appears that the sluggish flow is all at the surface; below, all is still, and the mud is allowed to settle and to become a hotbed of weeds and all kinds of vermin – like a selfish, lazy, purposeless kind of life, crying out against being disturbed or stirred up in any way; like some soul protecting itself lest any ray of light should pierce through and disturb its habitual way of life. As Dafydd Iwan's song says, 'Leave me alone, O my God, let me be!'

> 'Cleanse me with hyssop, and I shall be clean; wash me, and I shall be whiter than snow.'
> Psalm 51:7

> 'I will turn my hand against you; I will thoroughly purge away your dross and remove your impurities.'
> Isaiah 1:25

> 'For whoever wants to save his life will lose it, but whoever loses his life for me will find it.'
> Matthew 16:25

14
DEVOTION

Meeting during days of shearing,
Boasting of the sheepdogs' skill,
Living by the mountain torrent,
Dying by the murmuring rill.

That, in translation, is Eifion Wyn's description of the shepherd's life. A diffident dislike of appearing to boast is the only thing that keeps many a shepherd from recounting stories by the dozen of the wisdom of his dog and its devotion to its work. Some interesting stories have come from Scotland about the famous sheep-dog known as the Border Collie. There is one remarkable account which takes us back a good many years.

A farmer from Peebles, to the south of Edinburgh, had bought some sheep from another farm a good way off. All by herself, his faithful dog started out to drive the sheep to her own home on the other side of the mountain – and that, be it remembered, at a time when there were not many boundaries in existence.

Her master was tempted to linger awhile, over his pint perhaps, with the vendor. When he returned home later on that evening, he realized to his consternation that the sheep and the dog had not arrived. In real anxiety he and his son set out in different directions to look for them. But what did the farmer see almost immediately coming to meet him but the flock of sheep with the dog behind them – and in her mouth a new-born puppy, still wet from the womb!

On her way home, the expectant mother had given birth to her pups. She had delivered herself of them while keeping the sheep together lest they mix with other sheep on the mountain. Then, when she was able to resume her duties and the responsibility of bringing the sheep home, she picked up one member of the little family in her mouth, to bring him with her to the shelter of the farm.

When she had finished the work of getting the flock safely into the fold, she made a warm, snug nest and laid the pup in it. Then she disappeared into the darkness, and reappeared later with a second pup in her mouth, and then a third. When she arrived back with the fourth, the poor little thing was dead!

Her duty and faithfulness to her master and her work came first in her life. It was as though she were consecrated, as though she had dedicated her life to please her master and to do his will before considering her own instincts.

O for such a dedication to our Heavenly Master!

15
THE SECOND ATTEMPT

'I'll never bring the car to Cardiff again!' I could just make out what John was muttering under his breath. (I still don't know whether I was meant to hear or not.) We had just discovered that we had taken the wrong road yet again – this time as we were leaving Cardiff. Now, every sign we saw told us that we were making for Merthyr Tydfil and not for Newport as we intended.

Well! well! we wondered, feeling somewhat ashamed of ourselves, how on earth could we have misunderstood the instructions we had been given? It would not be easy to admit our stupidity to the one who had directed us.

Every turn of the wheels was taking us further in the wrong direction and, with the realization of our mistake, all the pleasure of motoring was completely gone. There was nothing for it now but to be on the watch for the first possible way off this road.

At length an exit came in sight. How thankful we were to escape from the unceasing mad rush of the dual carriageway. It gave us the opportunity to study again the instructions given us on the back of an envelope before we started out.

Our first reaction was to blame each other. That got us nowhere! Next, we tried to comfort each other by putting the blame on our advancing years (loath though we are, as a rule, to admit to this!). Then we blamed the instructions – not enough warning given of all the wrong turnings that two innocent country folk like ourselves might be tempted to take.

While we were sadly beginning to accept the idea that we would never again come to our beloved Cardiff in our own car, we were gradually enveloped by a wave of relief as we realized that the chief reason for our confusion was that we had no map of the city and its environs.

If we had a map to pore over we could see our present position quite clearly. We would understand the direction perfectly, where each road led, and what to expect on each of them, instead of being entirely dependent on the directions of others – some detailed, localized outline of the road from this person or that.

That is what comes of taking advice from people in a bus queue, who often have no experience at all of driving

a car. Those who are long familiar with the neighbourhood are often not the best to help either; they know their
surroundings too well to count the number of traffic-lights
to go through before changing direction, or how many
exits to ignore when turning off a roundabout – their
usual sign or landmark is some building or other.

Yes, it is by studying the whole map that we get the
complete picture. It is a dangerous thing in life to allow
ourselves to be led by isolated texts from the Bible, often
out of the context of the rest of the passage. How
important it is for us to be guided by the whole truth as it
is found in the Word of God!

That day in Cardiff we had to go back to the place
where we had taken the wrong turning in order to find the
right road once more. And the same is true when we are
convicted and corrected by the truth.

Take Abram for instance. What Abram did was to go
back to the place where God had last been real to him. He
had taken the wrong turning and gone down to Egypt to
escape the distress of the famine, and there he had lied
and denied his wife.

But Abram came back from Egypt: 'He went from
place to place until he came to Bethel, to the place
between Bethel and Ai where his tent had been earlier and
where he had first built an altar. There Abram called on
the name of the Lord' (Genesis 13:3-4).

'Direct my footsteps according to your word; let no
sin rule over me.'
Psalm 119:133

'In his heart a man plans his course, but the Lord
determines his steps.'
Proverbs 16:9

'Your word is a lamp to my feet and a light for my path.'
Psalm 119:105

How precious is the Book divine,
By inspiration given!
Bright as a lamp its doctrines shine,
To guide our souls to heaven.

O'er all the strait and narrow way
Its radiant beams are cast;
A light whose ever-cheering ray
Grows brightest at the last.

This lamp through all the tedious night
Of life shall guide our way,
Till we behold the clearer light
Of an eternal day.

JOHN FAWCETT

16
MARKING
THE SHEEP

'A Welsh sheep [or some other breed] has strayed on to this farm. If it is not claimed within ten days, it will be sold to cover the costs.'

This kind of notice is often to be seen in our local papers. And, of course, if there is no further description of the animal added to this, no one will trouble to go and see it, and to find the owner will be impossible. In fact, this is nothing but a way of keeping the animal without breaking the law. Another time the details of the marks on the one ear of the stray will be given, with the request that the owner describe the marks on the other. But if the finder is truly anxious to return the sheep to the owner, he must declare a full description of the marks on both ears.

Every sheep-owner will put his own special earmark on his sheep. These marks belong to the farm in perpetuity; if the farm is sold, they are sold with it. The mark on the fleece may be changed at will, but the mark on the ear is there to stay, it must never be changed. As many as thirty different ear-markings or cuttings are to be found within the compass of three counties in North Wales, and they are used in some two thousand different combinations – and all this to protect the rights of the owner.

While the lambs are quite young, a mark will be put on their fleece. As they grow in the course of the year, this mark will grow with them and become less distinct. As the lambs rub themselves in the peaty soil of their environment, push their way through thickets of thorn and briers, and endure the hard storms of winter, so the mark in their coats gets fainter and fainter; and eventually of course, when they are sheared, it disappears altogether. Still, this mark can easily be reprinted on the wool; it is a superficial thing, easy to put on and easy to lose.

With regard to the earmarks however – the cuts made on the ears of the young lambs – it is a different story.

These will grow as the lamb grows, and become more and more distinct. The same is true of names carved on the trunk of a young tree; as the tree grows, so the letters become thick-lipped and obvious. If the mark is made correct and clear on the sheep's ear at the outset, it will be as clear at the end of its life as when it was a year old.

There is an earmark which entails splitting the ear lengthwise. When this particular earmark is cut, there is always the possibility that the two edges of the split will stick to each other and become firmly healed together again. This has often been the cause of trouble when the owner has tried to claim his sheep, or in a court case where a man is accused of sheep-stealing. Strangely enough, the evidence of the earmark is infallible even then. The truth will always emerge when the ear is turned inside out, for the traces of the scar remain! Once the earmark of the master is on the sheep, it is there for ever.

In order that the mark may be identical on every sheep, it is usual for the master to cut the ears of his flock himself. In that way he can immediately recognize his own cuts, and identify his own property whether at home or astray.

To be earmarked is not a painless ordeal for the lamb, of course. Yet if it is to be one with the rest of the flock, the price must be paid. And who is not moved with pity to see the sides of the poor little heads red with the blood running from the cut ears?

We would be glad to spare the sweet innocent little things such pain, but that is the price to pay for belonging to the flock, and each must pay it for himself.

'I will write on him the name of my God . . . and I will also write on him my new name.'
      Revelation 3:12

'And his name will be on their foreheads.'
  Revelation 22:4

'I give them eternal life, and they shall never perish;
no-one can snatch them out of my hand.'
  John 10:28

17
THE CIRCLE

It is essential for the owner of a mixed farm to divide his interests and his duties equally – well, that is, as far as it is possible to do so. His various responsibilities should form a circle in his life, and the ideal is to be ready at all times for each task as it comes in its turn within that circle.

The changing seasons of the year bring changes in the work-pattern in their wake. And it is very easy to become obsessed by the very newness of that change of work and your interest in it, and to be completely swallowed up in it to the exclusion of all else. At lambing time, the temptation is to neglect the cows, whose feeding and care have been a heavy responsibility throughout the winter. Now, the duties towards the inhabitants of the byre tend to become a burden. But one dare not forget, be it summer or winter, that difficulties with calving, or trouble with the udders, can mean a very considerable loss, as well as much pain and discomfort to the black cattle.

That is what makes life on a mixed farm so interesting – the constant variety in the work. And the secret of success is never to let yourself be swallowed up by one responsibility at the expense of neglecting the other. When the well-being of the sheep is very close to the shepherd's heart, it is easy to overestimate the importance of their injections (especially today, when there are so many remedies to be had for the various ailments) and to neglect the injecting of oil into the joints of the tractor and the machine family. After all, the loss of a sheep is not to be compared with the loss sustained in losing a machine! At the same time there is real heart-break in losing the mother of a lamb, say, from a calcium deficiency, and that because of a failure to reach her in time to correct the defect with an injection. For with this complaint any disturbance or commotion will suddenly result in loss of consciousness and death.

Besides the great care that must be taken at lambing time to keep the lambs alive, it is essential to provide pasture and sustenance for them so that they may grow steadily. There must be some degree of understanding concerning the condition of the land, how to treat it and feed it, for the soil will differ from one district to another. Then, to avoid future troubles and to ensure a happy neighbourhood, the boundaries must receive attention; and in this connection must be mentioned the special craft of hedge-weaving, which can easily absorb all one's attention.

And then there is harvest time, a very difficult season in which to share attention and responsibility fairly. Good weather for reaping the crop can be lacking in many a year. But when the weather is wet and humid, the black flies and the bluebottles will be at their busiest, blowing their maggot eggs into the sheep's woolly coats. If they are not dealt with promptly and speedily, it can mean great financial loss, and much unnecessary suffering to the sheep.

The mark of a good workman is, doubtless, that he is wholly absorbed in his work; but if he is the owner of a mixed farm, he must also divide his time and his interests. He must try to remember everything – work, prices and market trends, and all the various aspects of husbandry. To make the circle and the responsibility into a perfect whole, the greatest of all the virtues is the ability to keep a balance between the practical and the theoretical, between the work of the hand and the work of the head.

A similar perfect roundness belongs to the life of the believer. If we want to convince the world that we have new life in Christ, the fruit of the Spirit must be evident in its full-orbed entirety – 'love, joy, peace, patience, kindness, goodness, faithfulness, gentleness and self-control' (Galatians 5:22-23). These virtues must form the whole circle of our lives, a circle without a break. Yes, and all these things must be present in the circle at the same time.

'For this very reason, make every effort to add to your faith goodness; and to goodness, knowledge; and to knowledge, self-control; and to self-control, perseverance; and to perseverance, godliness; and to godliness, brotherly kindness; and to brotherly kindness, love. For if you possess these qualities in increasing measure, they will keep you from being ineffective and unproductive in your knowledge of our Lord Jesus Christ. But if anyone does not have them, he is near-sighted and blind, and has forgotten that he has been cleansed from his past sins.

'Therefore, my brothers, be all the more eager to make your calling and election sure. For if you do these things, you will never fall, and you will receive a rich welcome into the eternal kingdom of our Lord and Saviour Jesus Christ.'

2 Peter 1:5-11

'Now that you know these things, you will be blessed if you do them.'

John 13:17

18
OUT OF DARKNESS INTO LIGHT

In the early summer, as the earth begins to show signs of life and just enough grass has appeared for the cows to get their tongues around it, the day comes for them and their calves to be turned out to taste it. This is bliss for every little calf, for now he can suck his mother and quench his thirst whenever he likes – with her permission, of course.

During the winter the calves are shut in together in a shed, and are only set free morning and evening to visit their mothers in the byre. What a scramble when the door at the far end of the byre is opened! Such a hurry to get the teats into their mouths, their four legs flailing in every direction, so slippery is the floor! They are down doing the splits one minute and up the next; heading for their mother's udder, butting her and slipping and slobbering until the froth begins to dribble from their mouths. It is difficult to convince them that they have exhausted the supply available for that meal, and they are reluctant to admit that they are satisfied; they will use all their ingenuity to avoid going back to their quarters in that dark shed.

But now the day has dawned for them to be freed. Their mothers have already been let loose, and now the door of the shed is opened for the calves to follow them. The cows go straight to the far end of the yard, for they are used to being turned out every day, and one would think that the calves would take advantage of the open door to leap to freedom. But no! In spite of being pushed from behind, you would think that there was something wrong with all four legs, or that they were held back by four-wheel brakes that could not be released!

There is no point in using a stick or any form of force; the front legs are like poles planted firmly in the earth. One might as well stop pushing when it avails nothing! The cows must be fetched back from the far end of the yard to persuade their calves to come out. They must be coaxed out into the light. They have to be convinced, in their own language and by the behaviour of the cows, that things are so much better outside. It is always those who have learned to enjoy freedom and light themselves who can recommend the light effectively to those who are more accustomed to darkness.

And now they venture out, very cautiously and carefully, each one pressing close to its mother. Oh! what a big, strange world the yard seems to the little calf who until now has measured nothing more than the length of its shed and the byre. They appear quite stunned as they look around. Little by little they begin to get used to things, and by the time they reach the field their legs are beginning to obey them. Up go their tails and they are away at a run! Well, well! Talk about liberty and licence! Now the game is to know the full length and breadth of the field – and the height of the hedges! Some run in all directions to discover for themselves what the great world has to offer them. Some go eastward to see what they can find, and some go to the west; but soon they all settle down happily in the freedom and the light, as those who are fully convinced that nothing in the whole world can offer them anything better than this.

'This is the verdict: Light has come into the world, but men loved darkness instead of light.'
John 3:19

'For he has rescued us from the dominion of darkness and brought us into the kingdom of the Son he loves.'
Colossians 1:13

'For you were once darkness, but now you are light in the Lord.'
Ephesians 5:8

'It is for freedom that Christ has set us free. Stand firm, then [in that freedom].'
Galatians 5:1

Long my imprisoned spirit lay
    Fast bound in sin and nature's night;
Thine eye diffused a quickening ray,
    I woke, the dungeon flamed with light;
My chains fell off, my heart was free,
I rose, went forth, and followed Thee.

CHARLES WESLEY

19
WILD OATS

It is a grievous blow for a farmer to find wild oats
growing in his corn, whether full-grown or in the early
stages. For advice on how to destroy them, he is urged to
get in touch with the Ministry of Agriculture immediately.
Many a chemical for their destruction is advertised on the
market, but it is necessary to take great care in using
weed-killer, for it can so easily ruin the value of the crop
for man and beast. And, in addition, its effectiveness only
lasts for one season's growth.

The problem in this country has shown an alarming increase in these past few years, and equally so in Europe and America. Indeed there are few grain-producers who are not, to some degree, faced with this problem.

Once the seed becomes mixed with the grain, it is difficult, if not impossible, to separate the two. Furthermore, the crop can no longer be sold as seedcorn, nor as grain to be ground into flour, not even flour for the animals. In the world of grain production this is the most harmful of all weeds. The seeds of the wild oats can remain in the soil for as long as six years without showing any growth, provided they are not disturbed or upturned to the surface. In addition, the seeds are easily scattered abroad to other fields and farms by birds, and also in the soil carried by machines and tractors constantly on the move from farm to farm.

This worthless growth was found in our hay recently. It is possible that it came with straw that we bought from England, and was then spread over the fields in the animals' droppings. There is no nourishment in this deceitful crop; it does nothing but impoverish the soil. It sheds its seeds very early on, before the hay can be harvested or the corn gathered in, and those seeds remain in the soil to produce even more the following year. But all this is no problem for us, compared with the nuisance caused to a farmer who is almost exclusively a grain-producer.

The great difficulty is to recognize it in order to destroy it. According to the Ministry, the best way of getting rid of it is to pull the young growth out by the roots before its seeds are scattered, and that by hand – yes, even in this mechanical age! This, by the way, is the direct opposite of the parable of the tares, which have to be left until the harvest. But unlike the tares in the parable, our main problem is that the young growth is so like the corn that it is very difficult to distinguish the one from the other. If the grain has been drilled, this uninvited weed is usually found growing between the rows of good grain; and if the growth of the corn is slow and weak, it will encourage the weed to make the most of its opportunity to grow.

It is somewhat easier to recognize when the crop has grown a little, as it is usually that much taller than the wheat or the barley. But the ideal time to uproot it is when the young corn shoot develops two leaves. At that point the weed differs from the wheat and the barley. The leaves of the latter turn in a clockwise semi-circle, while the leaf of the wild oats turns in the opposite direction. But having said this, it takes close inspection and an exceptionally keen eye to recognize it amongst the other growth, and it is a laborious exercise to uproot and burn it all. This weed, like many another, knows that its only hope of continuance is to imitate the true growth as closely as it can.

This too is one of the wiles of the Evil One – that is, to imitate the true, to make the false as like as possible to the truth. From the beginning his work has been to deceive and to blind. A keen discernment is needed to differentiate between true and false, and one of the gifts of the Holy Spirit is the gift of 'the ability to distinguish between spirits' (1 Corinthians 12:10). When such a variety of human ideas and heretical religions is offered to us, and that often on our very doorstep, this is an important gift, and one to be earnestly desired.

'No-one can say, "Jesus is Lord," except by the Holy Spirit.'
    1 Corinthians 12:3

'Dear friends, do not believe every spirit, but test the spirits to see whether they are from God, because many false prophets have gone out into the world.'

1 John 4:1

20
THROUGH
DEEP WATERS

The very word 'scab' is hateful to the sheep farmer; it brings back memories like nightmares from the past. It is a disease that attacks the skin of the sheep, caused by a certain kind of parasitic mite. When a sheep suffers from 'scab', these minute creatures, in every stage of development from eggs to adult, are certain to be present at the same time.

The lesion may be seen on any area of skin, including the head and inside the ear. It does not attack any other animal. The diagnostic sign is that the sheep scratch themselves, chiefly around the shoulder and the tail area, leaving bald patches. When this is observed the farmer is required to inform the Ministry vet at once.

There were no cases of the disease in Britain for twenty years, but it reappeared in England in 1972, and in Wales the following year. In an effort to rid the country of it, a law is now in force which requires that the whole flock be gathered together, and every single sheep, without exception, be completely submerged for a few seconds – head and all – and kept for one minute in a bath containing a solution of benzine hexachloride, conforming to the Ministry of Agriculture's instructions.

It appears that this mixture, when made up according to official instructions, is strong enough to ensure that one dip is enough to kill the eggs. But the last time this particular misfortune befell us, we had to gather the sheep together and put each one through the treatment *twice* within fourteen days – and that during the busy period of the hay harvest! And there stood a policeman supervising proceedings with his watch – one or two wags felt like pushing him and his watch into the tub!

One cannot but feel sorry for the poor sheep, thrown so suddenly and unceremoniously into the bath – thrown in on their backs, for the wool opens out better that way. If one of them succeeds in swimming the length of the bath with its head above water, there will be someone with a wooden pole ready to push it under, so that the whole of it – ears, mouth, nose and all – disappears out of sight into the disinfectant.

When the rams with their curly horns reach the far end of the tub, they no doubt suppose that the treatment is over; but without warning the long pole is hooked into the curve of their horns and they are pulled back to the start and plunged once more into the solution. All this is very necessary, for the root of the horns is a good hiding-place for the seeds of maggots and scab. And then what sneezing and shaking of heads and scattering of water-drops from the fleeces, when once they feel their feet on the firm ground of the drying pen!

They take it all so meekly – 'as a sheep before her shearers is silent' (Isaiah 53:7). If an occasional ram knew his strength, the dipper would often be with him in the dipping bath!

Innocent creatures! If only there were some way of letting them know why they must endure such treatment, that they might know the purpose of it all, that it is for their good, and to save them from future suffering! If only they might realize the love of the shepherd for them, which is responsible for it all!

The One in whom we trust, the Great Shepherd of the sheep, will sometimes ask us to go through a similar treatment, and often, like the sheep, we do not understand the reason for it. But it is all for our good.

'And we know that in all things God works for the good of those who love him, who have been called according to his purpose.'
Romans 8:28

'Jesus replied, "You do not realise now what I am doing, but later you will understand." '
    John 13:7

'No discipline seems pleasant at the time, but painful. Later on, however, it produces a harvest of righteousness and peace for those who have been trained by it.'
    Hebrews 12:11

21
HIS MASTER'S VOICE

'I wonder what will become of him,' we said to one another as we looked at the hairy little black and white bundle in the cardboard box. He had just joined us – a little five-week-old puppy – as an extra passenger in the car as we made our way home after our holiday in the Hebrides.

His pedigree was very much in his favour. Mac had sprung from one of the most renowned lines in the sheep-dog world, Wiston Cap. But ancestry and pedigree are not everything; it is all-important in a sheep-dog that he should have an intelligent personality, sensible and quick to understand what is expected of him. He might be head-strong, with a strong will of his own, too inflexible to bend to the will and command of his master. He might be overpowering in his handling of the sheep, upsetting them by glaring at them fiery-eyed.

His aim should be to win the confidence of the sheep and ensure their co-operation. He should be able to come right up to the sheep and even come among them, should it be necessary to separate them, without frightening them and scattering them in all directions. The secret is to master them without upsetting them, to create a kind of kinship with the sheep by making them feel that he knows what he is trying to do, without bumbling about in uncertainty or rushing around unnecessarily.

A good dog realizes that there is purpose in his every movement. Under the guidance of his master's voice, he knows that he will be moving to a pattern as his master tells him each movement in turn. No, he does not know the pattern, but he does know obedience – the obedience which comes from trust in his master.

The story of young dogs who have not begun to know their master's commands is always the same: their very instinct is for working with sheep, but there is no discipline. They run the sheep here, there and everywhere; it is all quite purposeless and energy-wasting. That is the way it is, before they learn to listen, to understand and to obey the one who can wisely master-mind the pattern.

We had to get rid of one young dog that developed the habit of taking his lead from the other dogs. He would always run with his eye on another dog, taking no notice of his master's direct command to himself. All his interest was in what the others were doing, and every effort to break him of the habit failed.

If you ever see me leaving the house like a bolt from the blue, you may be sure that I have seen a little group of sheep making a bee-line for my flowers in all the glory of their new bloom. One day someone had left the garden gate open! Mac, a very sensible dog by now, was lying on the back door-step. I shouted to him to help me drive them out at once, but away he went towards the old house with his tail between his legs, his whole bearing announcing that I had offended him deeply – and all so suddenly! I could not persuade him to come back. The more I tried to coax him, the further he went.

It took me some time to work out the reason for this, for he and I always seemed to be such great friends. He had misunderstood the tone of my voice and thought I was scolding him when in reality I was trying to persuade him to chase the sheep out. He did not spend enough time in my company to know and understand the difference between a rebuke and a command. He did not know my voice. He was not used to taking orders from me, only pampering.

The secret of it all is to live close enough to the Master to be able to recognize the tone of His voice and catch the merest whisper of His wishes.